I0821253

This Is Why You PEE

Dana Peabody

An imprint of PHOENIX International Publications, Inc.

Artwork © Shutterstock 2025 VaLiza; Retouch man; Pixoode; Ilmoto; bsd studio; AnyaLis; olllikeballoon; designemr; Marina Akinina; Prostock-studio; Littlekidmoment; fizkes; Andy Shell; New Africa; svtdesign; Kues; Ka Han; robuart; T-K-M; Tarasyuk Igor; Jfanchin; Jr images; Danny Smythe; Sudowoodo; mw_atp5; Katakari; RSH_GRAPHICS; Breyenn; Anna Sedneva; RTimages; JIANG HONGYAN; vitals; NaughtyNut; Fresh_Vector; Connect Images - Legacy; Arthur Simoes; Ching Louis Liu; stocksolutions; Russamee

Published by Sequoia Kids Media,
an imprint of Sequoia Publishing & Media, LLC

Sequoia Publishing & Media, LLC,
a division of Phoenix International Publications, Inc.

8501 West Higgins Road, Chicago, Illinois 60631
34 Seymour Street, London W1H 7JE
Heimhuder Straße 81, 20148 Hamburg

This edition is published by arrangement with BookLife Publishing

CustomerService@PhoenixInternational.com

www.PhoenixInternational.com

Library of Congress Control Number: 2024952912

ISBN: 979-8-7654-1136-0

This Is Why You PEE

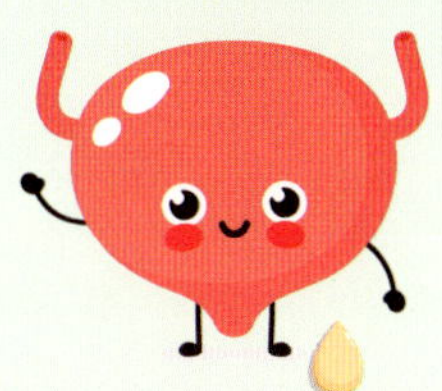

Table of Contents

Bold words are explained in the glossary.

Is your Bladder Bursting?

Are you hopping on the spot and quickly trying to find a bathroom? It sounds like you need to pee!

Don't hold it for too long!

When you need to pee, it's hard to think about anything else. But have you ever thought...

A Drink Goes In

We all need water to live. Our bodies do lots of different jobs all at once all the time. Water is needed to carry out lots of these jobs.

Gulp!
Gulp!
Gulp!

We can get water from lots of different things that we eat and drink.

Here are a few of the jobs our bodies need water for:

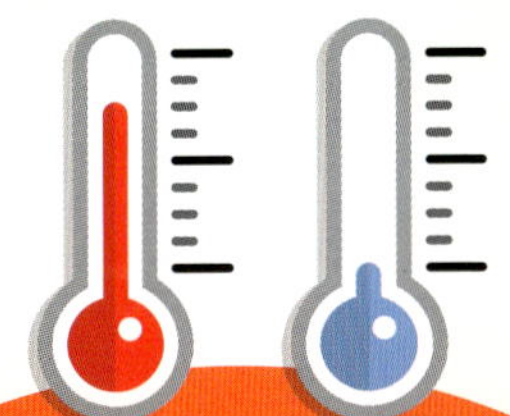

Keeping our bodies at the right temperature.

Helping us to fight off illnesses.

Carrying the things we need around our bodies in our blood.

In fact, every **cell** in your body needs water to work!

The Urinary System

We drink: we pee. But what comes out is very different from what goes in. The **liquid** we drink goes through lots of organs and other body parts before it becomes pee.

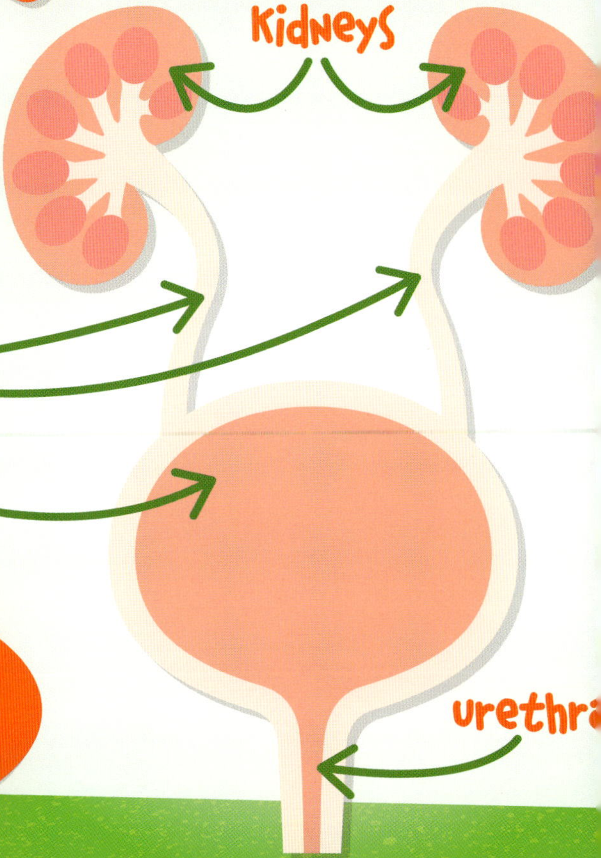

Kidneys

ureters

Bladder

urethra

Organs are parts of our body that have certain jobs.

All of these parts work together to control things such as:

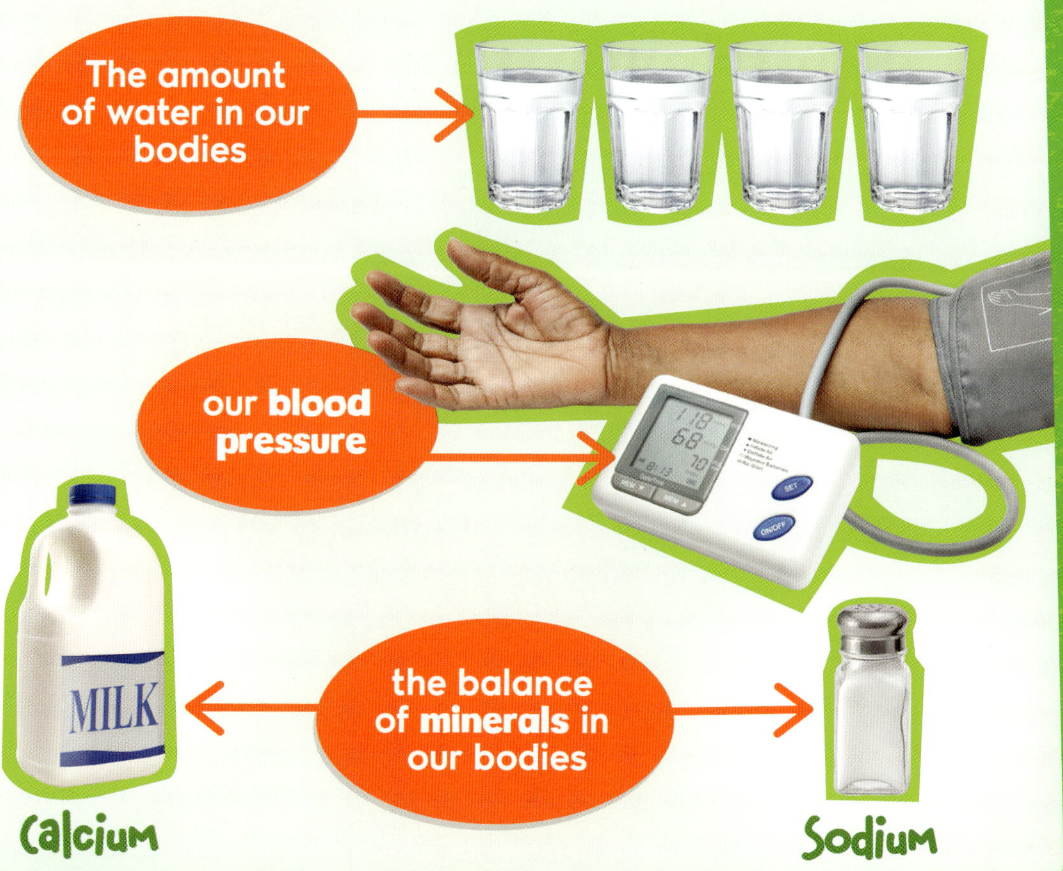

Journey of Pee

How does water become pee?

Step 1:

You drink the water and swallow it. It travels down the **esophagus** and into the STOMACH.

Step 2:

The water then travels through the INTESTINES. It is here that the water is **absorbed** into the cells and the bloodstream.

Step 3:

As your blood travels through your KIDNEYS, it gets **filtered**. Any extra water, waste, and **hormones** are taken out of the bloodstream.

Step 4:

The waste liquid is then taken from your KIDNEYS through your ureters and into your BLADDER.

Step 5:

The urine (pee) builds up in your BLADDER until you really need to...

Step 6:

PEE!

Pee Comes Out

We need to drink lots of water so that all of the bad things can be flushed out of our body.

You should try to drink around six to eight glasses of water a day.

As we digest and break down certain foods in our bodies, a waste product called urea is made. Foods rich in protein make urea. These include meat, **poultry**, and dairy.

Poultry

Dairy

Meat

Urea is one of the waste products that goes into pee.

Unwell Urine

Sometimes you may feel like you need to pee but can't go once you sit on the toilet. Sometimes it might even hurt to pee. This could mean you have a urinary tract infection, or a UTI for short.

Always tell an adult if it hurts to pee.

If you don't drink enough water, your pee may look very dark and smell very strong. This tells you that you are dehydrated (dee-hi-dray-ted).

Peculiar Pee

Sometimes food can change how our pee looks and smells.

Asparagus can make some people's pee smell stronger and turn slightly green.

Beets can make your pee a pinkish or red color.

Some food colorings in drinks and foods can make your pee different colors too.

Our pee can tell us a lot about our health. If your pee isn't normal, then there might be something wrong inside your body. If you have pee like this for more than a few days, tell a parent or caregiver.

The Pee Chart

We know that pee can come in a range of colors and shades. The color of our pee can let us know how hydrated we are.

0. 

No color

You might be drinking too much.

1. 

2. 

Pale yellow

You are well hydrated.

3. 

4.

5.

Yellow to dark yellow

You are getting a bit dehydrated. Have a drink of water.

6.

7.

8.

Orange to dark orange

You are very dehydrated. You need a drink now!

What color was your last pee?

How hydrated are you?

Pee Facts

Back in Roman times, people didn't have soap. To get their clothes clean, they used pee instead! They used pee from both humans and animals.

An adult bladder can hold 2–3 cups (500-700 milliliters) of pee at a time! But people can start to feel the need to pee when their bladder is about a quarter full.

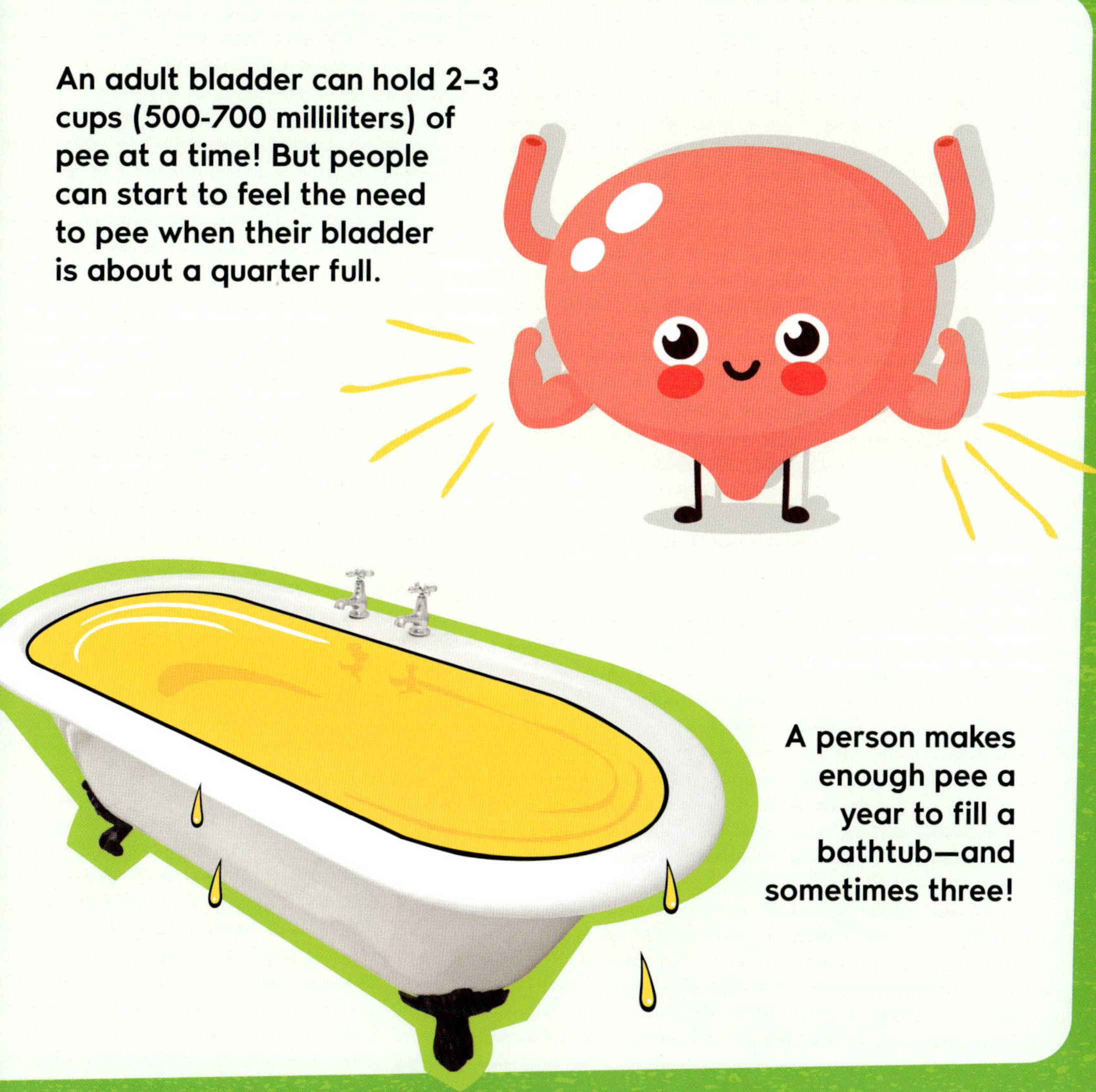

A person makes enough pee a year to fill a bathtub—and sometimes three!

What's in My Pee?

Whose pee could this be? Look for clues...

A.

B.

C.

D.

Answers: A. 2; B. 4; C. 1; D. 3

Glossary

absorbed: to have taken in or soaked up

blood pressure: how hard and fast blood is pumped around the body

cell: a basic unit that, when put together, makes up all living things

filtered: to remove unwanted materials by passing through something, like a sieve

hormones: chemicals in your body that tell cells what to do

liquid: a material that flows, such as water

minerals: important things that plants, animals, and humans need in order to grow

esophagus: a tube that connects your mouth to your stomach which food and water travel through

poultry: birds that are raised for meat and eggs, such as chickens

Index

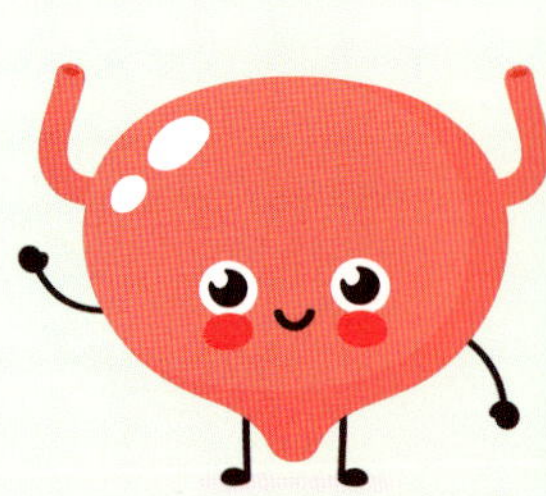